the PALEO
diet recipe book

Joy Skipper

B Bounty Books

First published in Great Britain in 2014 by
Hamlyn, a division of Octopus Publishing Group Ltd

This edition published in 2014 by Bounty Books,
a division of Octopus Publishing Group,
Carmelite House,
50 Victoria Embankment
London EC4Y 0DZ
www.octopusbooks.co.uk

Reprinted in 2016

An Hachette UK Company
www.hachette.co.uk

Copyright © Octopus Publishing Group Ltd 2014

ISBN: 978-0-753728-81-9

A CIP catalogue record for this book is available from the British Library

Printed and bound in China

Both metric and imperial measurements are given for the recipes. Use one set of
measures only, not a mixture of both.

Standard level spoon measurements are used in all recipes
1 tablespoon = 15 ml
1 teaspoon = 5 ml

Ovens should be preheated to the specified temperature. If using a fan-assisted
oven, follow the manufacturer's instructions for adjusting the time and temperature. Grills
should also be preheated.

This book includes dishes made with nuts and nut derivatives. It is advisable for those with
known allergic reactions to nuts and nut derivatives and those who may be potentially
vulnerable to these allergies, such as pregnant and nursing mothers, invalids, the elderly, babies
and children, to avoid dishes made with nuts and nut oils.

The Department of Health advises that eggs should not be consumed raw. This book contains
some dishes made with raw or lightly cooked eggs. It is prudent for more vulnerable people
such as pregnant and nursing mothers, invalids, the elderly, babies and young children to avoid
uncooked or lightly cooked dishes made with eggs.

CONTENTS

INTRODUCTION

This book will introduce you to the concept of the Paleolithic diet, which is believed to have been eaten by our ancestors thousands of years ago. Also known as the Paleo diet or the hunter–gatherer diet, it includes any food that could be hunted or found, such as meats, fish, nuts, leafy greens and seeds.

The Paleo diet is based on the concept that the best diet is the one to which we are genetically adapted, with the premise that human genetics have hardly changed since the dawn of agriculture. Research has shown that the aged populations of hunter–gatherer societies were virtually free of high cholesterol, diabetes, obesity, hypertension and other chronic diseases that have become endemic in Western societies. There are signs that indicate that our modern diet (full of refined foods, trans fats and sugar) is the root of most degenerative diseases, including cancer and heart disease, depression and fertility problems. We have changed our diets, but our genetics have not changed enough to accommodate them.

Over the past couple of years a number of books have written about the Paleo diet, each one with slightly different recommendations. In a way this is understandable – because they lived so long ago, it is difficult to be certain about what Paleo people ate or how they lived. What is clear is that the Paleo diet would have been based around a much more nutrient-dense, toxin-free, whole-food diet than the one that is eaten today. The best way to think of the diet is as a particular approach to eating, with a template that can be adjusted to suit each individual's biochemical needs. It is also important to think of it not so much as a diet, but as a healthy eating regime that can be maintained for life.

HOW TO USE THE BOOK

This book explains the basics of the Paleo diet, gives lots of tips and ideas to help you get started, and includes more than 100 recipes to incorporate into your everyday life. The great thing about the diet is that once you know what you can and cannot eat, there is nothing else to worry about! No calorie counting, no weighing of foods – the foods you are allowed can be eaten as often as you wish. The only foods that need to be limited are root vegetables and fruit (see page 17), as these are high in starch and sugar, and if excess sugar is not burned off it will turn to fat.

The recipes included here feature only the allowed foods, and these can be used to make meals and snacks throughout the day. Each one will give you ideas about how to use the many foods available on the Paleo diet – so, as long as you stick to those foods, you can also experiment with your own recipes.

So what can you eat? Well, anything that the hunter–gatherer would have been able to forage for – meats (Paleolithic man would have found wild meat, so the leanest cuts you can find are best), fish and seafood, vegetables, fruits, eggs, nuts and seeds. You can also reduce your toxin intake by choosing nutrient-dense organic foods. Foods to avoid include all grains, legumes and pulses, dairy and refined sugars (see page 12).

The Paleo diet is one that can be followed for life, not just as a short-term weight-loss regime. It is a healthy, long-term eating regime that has been shown to reduce a number of modern diseases.

IS THE PALEO DIET FOR EVERYONE?

There is no such thing as an optimal diet for the whole world – think of the Inuit or Masai who eat high-fat diets, yet remain healthy. So we should remember that our ancestors didn't all eat the same diet – there was a wide variation in the proportion of protein, carbohydrate and fat consumed, and the different types of food consumed by different populations around the world.

We are all unique, with individual lifestyles, and have grown up in different environments, with different toxin exposures and different experiences. So while many of our genes are the same, others are not, and the way some of them may have been expressed (the process by which information from a gene is used, converting it first into messenger DNA and then into a protein) may also be different. So the Paleo diet is about finding a diet that works for you.

If you have been using a diet based on significant amounts of processed food over a number of years, perhaps combined with high alcohol and toxin intake, the transition to a nutrient-dense, low-toxic diet may not be a smooth one. This doesn't mean that the Paleo diet is not for you, but you may have some work to do on improving your digestive system or other systems in the body to ensure that you are digesting and detoxifying optimally before you embark on the diet. Remember there is no such thing as a quick fix, especially if you have been on a heavily processed food diet for a long time.

Two groups of people that may struggle with this diet are vegetarians and vegans – this is because the hunter–gatherer diet includes meat, poultry, fish and eggs. And without legumes and grains, vegetarians and vegans will not be able to sustain a balanced diet with sufficient protein intake. See more on this on page 8.

HOW DOES THE DIET WORK?

A Paleo diet is naturally lower in carbohydrate than the modern diet and automatically eliminates many foods that are low in nutrients and high in calories. It will also eliminate processed foods that are high in hidden sugars, fats and toxins, and reduce the intake of foods that may cause intolerances or allergies, or foods that may be hard to digest. The carbohydrates on the Paleo diet (consisting of fruit and vegetables) are also low glycaemic index (GI) foods, meaning that they cause slow and limited rises in your blood sugar and insulin levels. Your body's blood sugar balance may be improved, as you will be eating more protein and good fat that will sustain your appetite for longer.

HEALTH BENEFITS

There are a number of reasons why the Paleo diet is healthy. Looking at it as a whole, and considering that the body is made up of protein, carbohydrates and fats, it makes sense that if you feed your body those nutrients in the cleanest form possible, then it will perform better.

We've already mentioned the benefits of cutting out toxins and increasing your intake of nutrient-dense foods. By eliminating processed foods, you are automatically eating a low-sodium diet while increasing your intake of potassium (rich in many vegetables, nuts and seeds), and the combination of low sodium and high potassium is a recipe for good vascular health and low blood pressure.

Clinical trials have shown that a Paleo diet may lower the risk of cardiovascular disease, blood pressure and markers of inflammation, help with weight loss, reduce acne and promote optimum health and athletic performance.

THE PALEO DIET AND EXERCISE

As with all healthy eating plans, you will see better results if you are active while on the diet. Hunter–gatherers were physically active on a daily basis as they sought food, water and shelter. We no longer have to do these things, but taking regular exercise is beneficial both for weight loss and for long-term health. If you are intending to follow the Paleo diet and have not been taking regular exercise, then it is advisable to seek help from a medical professional and get some advice on the level of exercise you should start with.

If you are a training athlete, you may be wondering if this diet will suit you. Not so long ago, carbohydrates were the endurance nutrient of choice, and protein was the focus of all body builders and strength athletes, but things have moved on since then. The Paleo diet is naturally high in animal protein, which is the richest source of branched-chain amino acids, which are needed for building and repairing muscles. It also reduces muscle loss because the diet is very alkaline (one way the body neutralizes an acid-producing diet is by breaking down muscle). The high intake of vegetables and fruit also ensures a high intake of vitamins, minerals and phytochemicals (natural chemical compounds), which help to support the immune system, an important issue for all athletes.

WHAT TO EXPECT ON THE DIET

If your present diet is high in processed foods, coffee, alcohol, wheat and dairy, it may take you a while to adjust to the Paleo diet and to find the foods that work for you. Keeping a food diary from day one may be helpful with this, as it is hard to remember retrospectively how you felt after eating something and if any foods affected you in any way. You may also get withdrawal symptoms from cutting out some of the old foods, so it could be a while before you start to feel better and see your body shape change.

GETTING STARTED

If you find the thought of a 'diet' a bit daunting, start by setting yourself a time challenge. Commit to a 30-day period where you eliminate the foods suggested below, therefore reducing toxins and food sensitivities, and so reducing allergic reactions. Then you can introduce the new foods that may have been absent from your diet, which may hopefully improve digestion, boost energy, regulate sugar balance and normalize weight. Once you start to get to grips with your new eating regime you may find some foods agree with you more than others, so you can start to tailor the diet to suit your individual needs.

Here is a basic list of foods to eat and not to eat:

To eat
- Grass-produced meats (grain causes the same problem in animals as it does in humans)
- Fish (wild is best, to avoid mercury and other toxins found in farmed fish)
- Seafood
- Fresh fruit (limit the amount if you are trying to lose weight as it is high in natural sugar)
- Fresh vegetables
- Eggs (look for omega-3 enriched)
- Nuts
- Seeds
- Healthy oil – olive, flaxseed, avocado, coconut, walnut

Don't eat
- Legumes (including peanuts) and pulses
- Dairy
- Cereal grains
- Refined sugar
- Potatoes
- Processed foods
- Salt

10 WAYS TO MAKE THE PALEO DIET WORK FOR YOU

1 Be organised
Spend time at the beginning of the week to shop and prepare food for the week ahead.

2 Plan ahead
Plan your meals in advance so you have something tasty to look forward to, so that you don't get hungry and reach for the wrong foods.

3 Take foods with you
If you work away from home, make yourself delicious lunches to take with you.

4 Restock the cupboards and fridge
Only have Paleo foods in the house – that way, you will never be tempted to cheat!

5 Veggie box delivery
Sign up to a veggie box delivery scheme to ensure you are eating fresh organic vegetables each week. You may even get to try some new ones you didn't know you liked.

6 Keep it simple
With each meal or snack, first include protein (meat, poultry, fish or eggs), then add some vegetables or fruit.

7 Eat regularly
Don't let yourself get hungry. Eat little and often; having snacks, such as a small handful of nuts and seeds with a piece of fruit, will sustain you between meals.

8 Eat a rainbow!
Vegetables are loaded with essential vitamins, minerals, enzymes, antioxidants, fibre and water, all essential for optimum health. The colour of your fruit and vegetables is linked to the nutrients they include, so eat as many colourful fruit and veg a day as you can – variety is key.

9 Use the 80:20 rule
The 80:20 rule means that you can spend 80% of your time on the diet, and 20% being less strict. So If you find you have a day or night when you really cannot stick to the diet (for example, you are invited out to dinner), don't worry, just count it as your 20% of being non-Paleo for that week, and get right back on to the Paleo eating regime the next day.

10 Start a food diary
Keep a note of what you eat, how you feel and how you sleep. Hopefully over time you will see positive changes and may be able to relate them to foods you are consuming.

FREQUENTLY ASKED QUESTIONS

Can a vegetarian or vegan follow the Paleo diet?
Because the Paleo diet is based on what a hunter–gatherer would have caught/found, it naturally includes meat. If you want to try the diet but choose not to eat meat, you need to include protein in your diet. Most vegetarians or vegans will gain from eating legumes, cereals and pulses, but these foods contain anti-nutrients that may have a negative effect (see page 8, Why no beans?). This means that the Paleo diet is not advisable for vegetarians or vegans.

Is it suitable for children?
If you can get your child to eat enough vegetables, this diet is fine for children – they really don't need all the refined carbohydrates (pizza, pasta etc.) to enable them to grow, because they can get carbohydrates (along with fibre, vitamins and minerals) from vegetables.

Is it suitable during pregnancy?
As the diet is rich in fresh fruit, vegetables, organic meat and fish it is fine to use during pregnancy.

How will I get my intake of calcium for my bones without dairy?

Bone health is mainly dependent on an acid/alkaline dietary balance. If the acid in the body is too high, then calcium is 'pulled' from the bones to neutralize it. Acid-producing foods include cheese, grains, legumes and salted foods, whereas fruit and vegetables are alkaline, so increasing these in your diet should bring the acid/alkaline, and therefore the calcium, back into balance. Leafy green vegetables, such as kale, and some nuts (almonds) and seeds (sesame) are also rich in calcium.

Is organic food really better for you?

There is constant debate about this, but research has shown that foods that have had to battle the elements to survive and grow without the help of pesticides and fertilizers are likely to be more nutrient-dense than those that had help.

Will I lose weight on the Paleo diet

If your present diet has been high in processed foods and refined carbohydrates there is a good chance that you may lose weight, as you will be eating foods that are easier for the body to recognize and digest.

How much fruit can I eat on the diet?

In general, fresh fruits are healthy foods that are good sources of minerals, vitamins and fibre. However, the fruits we eat today are sweeter, larger and contain less fibre than their wild counterparts, so if you are trying to lose weight it may be beneficial to limit high-sugar fruits, such as bananas, mangoes, grapes, apples, pineapples and kiwi fruits, and try to include more vegetables in your diet instead. Root vegetables, however, are higher in starch and sugar than leafy green vegetables, and so should be eaten in moderation, too.

Why no beans?

Beans contain lectins, which are carbohydrate-binding proteins present in most plants, especially seeds, beans and tubers like cereals, potatoes and beans. Until recently, their main use was as histology and blood transfusion reagents, but in the past two decades it has been realized that many lectins are toxic and inflammatory.

Which oils are allowed on the Paleo diet?

There are many different views on the kinds of oils that should be consumed when following the Paleo diet. The consensus, however, seems to be that oils from all the plants that are allowed can be consumed.

There are a number of options: olive oil (great for salads and sautéing, but don't heat too high); coconut oil (high in saturated fats but withstands high cooking temperatures so good for stir-fries); avocado oil (delicious in salad dressings or cooking at low temperatures); and sesame oil (very rich in flavour, so only a small amount is needed and it is not recommended as an everyday oil). Oils that should not be used are those rich in omega-6 fatty acids, plus oils from legumes or soy, such as groundnut oil, vegetable oil, sunflower oil, corn oil or rapeseed oil.

What can I drink and use instead of dairy milk?

Almond milk and coconut milk.

Can I eat peanuts on the Paleo diet?

No, they are legumes.

Some Paleo websites say you can have bacon and ham, and others don't – how to decide?

The diet is about eating the best quality, natural foods you can. Some bacons and hams may contain nitrates (even if it isn't on the label) and it has been suggested that these are not good for you. However, sodium nitrate when used to preserve these meats, is converted to sodium nitrite, a substance that occurs naturally in foods like spinach, carrots and celery. Remember that the word 'nitrate' refers to a compound made of nitrogen, which is the single biggest component of our atmosphere!

Is alcohol allowed on the diet?
Alcohol is not allowed on the diet, although if you like occasionally to add wine to food when you are cooking, just be sure that you burn off the alcohol.

Is the Paleo diet expensive?
The diet does not have to be expensive, especially if you normally buy pre-prepared food – cooking from scratch is not only healthier, but cheaper, too. Shop around to get the best prices, buy from local markets, and maybe even think about growing your own organic vegetables!

Can I get most of the ingredients at a supermarket?
Yes, all Paleo foods are readily available in supermarkets, including the fresh ingredients. If you have a good butcher and fishmonger nearby, you may also want to visit them to see what offers they have and get advice about cooking the best joints of meat or fresh fish.

Any tips for what to grab on the run?
Nuts, seeds and fruit are the easiest foods to carry around.

TOP TIPS FOR BEGINNERS

Sticking to a new eating regime can be difficult when there are outside influences, such as work or family, to juggle, too, so the following tips may be useful:

- Set small, achievable targets – try including a new food each week, or increasing your exercise by walking to a bus-stop that's further away from you normal one each morning.

- Get support – involve your family or friends by asking them to join you on the diet. That way, if you are cooking for the whole family you won't have to make separate meals, and everyone will benefit!

- Don't get hungry – ensure that you plan your day with sufficient healthy snacks so that you never get hungry; eating little and often is fine as long as it is based on the foods you are allowed. Maintain your appetite throughout the day, which will also help to keep your blood sugar balanced, causing less stress on the body. The less hungry you are, the easier it is to lose weight!

- Be aware of what you are eating – don't fall into the trap of 'mindless eating', just eating because food is there or has been offered. Eat in a conscious way, and savour each mouthful.

- Personalize the diet to suit you – it may take a few weeks for you to get to know which foods you like and those that work for you. You also have your own routine and it's important to make your diet work around that.

- Make changes that are sustainable – gradually change your diet to suit you and make sure the changes you make are those that can be maintained for life, not just for a few weeks.

1
BREAKFASTS

BLUEBERRY PANCAKES

These are perfect for a breakfast treat, and can be enjoyed without blueberries or with other berries stirred into the batter.

MAKES 12–14

Prep time: 12 minutes
Cooking time: 20 minutes

250 g (8 oz) sweet potato, chopped
200 g (7 oz) ground almonds
½ teaspoon baking powder
3 eggs, beaten
200 ml (7 fl oz) non-dairy milk
250 g (8 oz) blueberries
2 tablespoons olive oil
honey, to serve

• Cook the sweet potatoes in a pan of boiling water until tender. Drain and mash the potatoes, then transfer to a bowl and leave to cool slightly.

• Stir in the ground almonds and baking powder, then beat in the eggs and milk with a fork to give a thick batter. Finally, stir in 150 g (5 oz) of the blueberries.

• Heat ½ tablespoon olive oil in a frying pan and drop tablespoonfuls of the mixture into the pan to make 3–4 pancakes. Cook for 3–4 minutes until golden, then carefully flip over and cook for another 2–3 minutes.

• Remove the pancakes from the pan, keep warm and cook the remaining batter in the same way.

• Serve the pancakes with the remaining blueberries, and drizzle with honey.

SAMPHIRE OMELETTE

Otherwise known as 'poor man's asparagus', samphire is a delicious type of seaweed found along British coasts, especially those in Norfolk and Wales. It can be stir-fried as here, steamed or boiled, or served cold with a vinaigrette.

SERVES 1

Prep time: 5 minutes
Cooking time: 6–8 minutes

2 tbsp olive oil
2 spring onions, sliced
50 g (2 oz) samphire, woody ends
   trimmed
3 eggs
freshly ground black pepper

• Heat half the oil in a frying pan, add the spring onions and samphire and cook for 1 minute. Remove from the pan.

• Beat the eggs in a bowl with the black pepper and then mix in the spring onions and samphire.

• Heat the remaining oil in the frying pan and add the egg mixture, stirring it a little until it starts to set. Cook for a further 2–3 minutes, then gently fold the omelette in half and slide on to a warmed plate to serve.

SPICY PRAWN & ASPARAGUS EGGS

This filling and tasty breakfast of creamy scrambled eggs with prawns and asparagus will start your day off beautifully.

SERVES 4

Prep time: 10 minutes
Cooking time: 10 minutes

8 eggs
2 tablespoons non-dairy milk
pinch of paprika
freshly ground black pepper
150g (5 oz) asparagus, cut into 2.5 cm
   (1 inch) pieces
1 tablespoon olive oil
150 g (5 oz) cooked prawns

• Whisk the eggs lightly with the milk, paprika and pepper.

• Blanch the asparagus in boiling water for 2 minutes, then drain.

• Heat the olive oil in a frying pan, add the asparagus and prawns and cook for 1 minute before adding the eggs.

• Stir over a low heat to scramble the egg. Serve with a sprinkling of black pepper.

MELON COCKTAIL

Sometimes the simplest recipes are the best – all you need is good-quality ingredients that work well together. Be sure to use the ripest melon and the best flavoured honey.

SERVES 4

Prep time: 5 minutes

1 cantaloupe melon, cut into 4 wedges,
    seeds removed
large pinch ground ginger
1 tablespoon pecan nuts
1 tablespoon walnuts
2 tablespoons honey

• Sprinkle each of the melon wedges with a little ground ginger and leave to stand for 1–2 minutes.

• Toast the nuts and roughly break them over the melon slices. Drizzle each wedge with honey and serve.

SHASHOUKA

This North African dish is a good option if you like a spicy, substantial breakfast. It can also be served with a crisp green salad for lunch.

SERVES 4

Prep time: 8 minutes
Cooking time: 28–36 minutes

2 tablespoons olive oil
1 teaspoon cumin seeds
1 onion, sliced
1 garlic clove, crushed
1 red pepper, deseeded and sliced
1 yellow pepper, deseeded and sliced
a pinch of saffron
½ teaspoon smoked paprika
1 x 400 g (13 oz) tin chopped tomatoes
4 eggs
freshly ground black pepper

• Preheat the oven to 180°C (350°F), Gas Mark 4.

• Heat the oil in an ovenproof frying pan and cook the cumin seeds for 2 minutes before adding the onion. Cook for a further 3-4 minutes, until the onion starts to soften.

• Add the garlic and peppers and cook for another 3-4 minutes before adding the saffron, paprika and tomatoes. Cook for another 10–12 minutes.

• Make 4 wells in the mixture and crack an egg into each one. Sprinkle with black pepper.

• Place the pan in the oven and cook for 10–12 minutes until the egg is cooked but the yolk is still runny.

2

SOUPS AND SALADS

RED CABBAGE, ORANGE & CASHEW SALAD

This refreshing salad is full of crunch and a delightful citrus flavour – its cleansing taste will perfectly complement a simply grilled steak or grilled fish.

SERVES 2

Prep time: 10 minutes
Cooking time: 2 minutes

1 tablespoon cashew nuts
½ teaspoon cumin seeds
1 large orange, segmented
¼ small red cabbage, shredded
2 small carrots, peeled and grated
1 tablespoon chopped parsley
juice of 1 lemon
2 tablespoons extra virgin olive oil

• Toast the cashew nuts and cumin seeds for 2 minutes, then remove them from the heat.

• Toss together all of the ingredients and leave them to stand for 10 minutes at room temperature before serving, to allow the flavours to develop.

ANTIPASTI SALAD

A great, quick salad that can be made using pre-prepared jars of peppers and artichokes, or if you have more time you can roast your own!

SERVES 4

Prep time: 15 minutes

3 tablespoons extra virgin olive oil
juice of ½ lemon
½ teaspoon honey
1 garlic clove, crushed
2 hearts of Romaine lettuce, torn into bite-size pieces
1 red onion, thinly sliced
250 g (8 oz) roasted peppers, sliced
175 g (6 oz) artichoke hearts, halved
2 tablespoons olives
8 slices Parma ham
12 cherry tomatoes, halved
2 tbsp pine nuts, toasted
small bunch basil leaves, shredded

• Whisk together the oil, lemon juice, honey and garlic to make the dressing.

• Place the torn Romaine leaves on a large platter, then top with the remaining ingredients, finishing with the pine nuts and shredded basil leaves sprinkled over the top.

• Pour over the dressing and serve.

PRAWN, MANGO & AVOCADO SALAD

This salad is riot of colour and perfect for taking to a barbecue – you could even cook the prawns on the grill. Make sure your mango is perfectly ripe.

SERVES 4

Prep time:10 minutes

1 large mango, about 475 g (15 oz),
   peeled and stoned
1 ripe avocado, about 400 g (13 oz),
   peeled and stoned
2 large cos lettuces
16 large cooked king prawns, peeled
   but tails left on

DRESSING
juice of 2 limes
1 teaspoon honey
2 tablespoon vegetable oil
½ chilli, deseeded and finely chopped

• Cut the mango and avocado flesh into 2 cm (¾ inch) pieces. Discard the outer layer of leaves and cut the stems off the lettuces, leaving the hearts. Separate the leaves and add them to the mango and avocado with the prawns.

• Make the dressing by whisking together the lime juice, honey and oil with the chilli. Add the dressing to the salad, toss carefully to mix and serve immediately.

ASPARAGUS, QUAIL'S EGG & PARMA HAM SALAD

Asparagus and eggs are a perfect match, and these little quails' eggs always look so pretty in a salad, as well as tasting delicious!

SERVES 4

Prep time: 15 minutes
Cooking time: 4 minutes

750 g (1½ lb) asparagus, woody stems removed
12 quails' eggs
3 tablespoons extra virgin olive oil
juice of 1 lemon
1 teaspoon honey
125 g (4 oz) lamb's lettuce
2 heads chicory, roughly sliced
large bunch chives, snipped
8 slices Parma ham
freshly ground black pepper

• Steam the asparagus for 3–4 minutes until just tender. Refresh under cold water and slice in half.

• Meanwhile, softly boil the quails' eggs by gently placing them in a pan of boiling water, cooking for 3 minutes then refreshing under cold water to stop the cooking process. Peel off the shells when they are cool enough to handle.

• Whisk together the olive oil, lemon juice, honey and black pepper to make the dressing.

• Toss together the lamb's lettuce, chicory, chives and asparagus, pour over the dressing and toss again.

• Top with the slices of Parma ham and the halved poached quails' eggs.

CRISPY DUCK AND CASHEW SALSA

Duck has a lot of fat on it, but if it is cooked in the right way, it can have cris
skin and tender meat with lots of flavour.

SERVES 2

Prep time:15 minutes, plus marinating
Cooking time: 7–9 minutes

1 teaspoon sesame oil
1 teaspoon clear honey
1 teaspoon grated fresh root ginger
1 duck breast, about 150 g (5 oz), cut
   into strips
1 tablespoon cashew nuts
juice of ½ lemon
1 pak choi, chopped
1 carrot, peeled and grated
2 spring onions, sliced
¼ cucumber, cut into matchsticks
25 g (1 oz) bean sprouts

• Mix together the oil, honey and ginger in a bowl, then add th
duck strips and coat well. Leave to marinate for 5 minutes.

• Meanwhile, heat a dry nonstick frying pan over a medium-lo
heat and dry-fry the cashews for 3–4 minutes, shaking the pa
occasionally, until golden brown and toasted. Set aside.

• Heat a frying pan or griddle pan until hot, add the duck strip
(reserving the marinade) and cook for 4–5 minutes until crisp
and golden.

• Meanwhile, stir the lemon juice into the remaining marinade
make a dressing.

• Place the remaining ingredients in a large serving bowl and
toss together, then top with the duck. Serve drizzled with the
dressing.

DUCK, PEAR & POMEGRANATE SALAD

Although you can buy pomegranate molasses for the dressing, why not make your own? If you don't finish it, store for up to 2 weeks in the refrigerator.

SERVES 4

Prep time: 15 minutes
Cooking time: 15–20 minutes

2 large, lean duck breasts
2 Comice pears, cored and diced
125 g (4 oz) mixed leaf and herb salad
50 g (2 oz) walnut pieces
1 pomegranate, seeds removed

DRESSING
2 teaspoons lime juice
2 teaspoons raspberry vinegar
2 teaspoons pomegranate molasses
  (optional)
2 tablespoons walnut oil
salt and pepper

• Remove any excess fat from the duck breasts and score the surface using a sharp knife. Heat a ridged griddle pan until hot, then add the duck breasts, skin side down, and cook for 8–10 minutes. Turn them over and cook for a further 5–10 minutes or until cooked to the pinkness desired. Remove from the pan, cover with foil and leave to rest.

• Mix together the pears and leaf salad in a bowl. Arrange on serving plates and scatter with the walnut pieces.

• Whisk together all the dressing ingredients in a bowl and season to taste. Drizzle over the salad.

• Slice the duck breasts and arrange on the salad. Scatter over the pomegranate seeds and serve immediately.

TURKEY & AVOCADO SALAD

This salad makes a delicious addition to a picnic lunch rolled up in a lettuce leaf to make it easier to eat.

SERVES 4

Prep time: 20 minutes

375 g (12 oz) cooked turkey
1 large avocado
punnet of mustard and cress
150 g (5 oz) mixed salad leaves
50 g (2 oz) mixed toasted seeds, such
    as pumpkin and sunflower

DRESSING
2 tablespoons apple juice
2 tablespoons natural yogurt
1 teaspoon clear honey
1 teaspoon wholegrain mustard
salt and pepper

• Thinly slice the turkey. Peel, stone and dice the avocado and mix it with the mustard and cress and salad leaves in a large bowl. Add the turkey and toasted seeds and stir to combine.

• Make the dressing by whisking together the apple juice, yogurt, honey and mustard. Season to taste with salt and pepper.

• Pour the dressing over the salad and toss to coat.

ITALIAN BROCCOLI & EGG SALAD

The beautiful golden egg yolks and green broccoli make this a really pretty dish on the table. The tarragon adds a delicate aniseed flavour.

SERVES 4

Prep time:10 minutes
Cooking time:8 minutes

4 eggs
300 g (10 oz) broccoli
2 small leeks, about 300 g (10 oz) in total
sprigs of tarragon, to garnish (optional)

DRESSING
4 tablespoons lemon juice
2 tablespoons olive oil
2 teaspoons clear honey
1 tablespoon capers, drained
2 tablespoons chopped tarragon
salt and pepper

• Half-fill the base of a steamer with water, add the eggs and bring to the boil. Cover with the steamer top and simmer for 8 minutes or until hard-boiled.

• Meanwhile, cut the broccoli into florets and thickly slice the stems. Trim, slit and wash the leeks and cut them into thick slices. Add the broccoli to the top of the steamer and cook for 3 minutes, then add the leeks and cook for a further 2 minutes.

• Make the dressing by mixing together the lemon juice, oil, honey, capers and tarragon in a salad bowl. Season to taste with salt and pepper.

• Crack the eggs, cool them quickly under cold running water and remove the shells. Roughly chop the eggs.

• Add the broccoli and leeks to the dressing, toss together and add the chopped eggs. Garnish with sprigs of tarragon (if liked).

PEA & HAM SOUP

This soup is a wonderful opportunity to use up any leftover ham – you can use the bone to make the stock, too, so nothing goes to waste.

SERVES 4

Prep time: 8 minutes
Cooking time: 18 minutes

1 tablespoon olive oil
1 onion, chopped
1 litre (1¾ pints) ham or chicken stock
500 g (1 lb) frozen peas
350 g (11½ oz) cooked ham, shredded
freshly ground black pepper

• Heat the oil in a pan and sauté the onion for 3–4 minutes, until starting to soften.

• Pour in the stock and bring to the boil. Then pour in the peas and a small handful of the ham, bring the contents back to the boil and simmer for 3–4 minutes.

• Remove from the heat and, using a blender or food processor, blend until smooth.

• Season with black pepper and serve with the remaining ham stirred in.

THAI-STYLE BEEF SALAD

The chilli in this recipe really brings the ingredients to life. Choose the highest-quality grass-fed beef you can find for the best flavour.

SERVES 4

Prep time: 15 minutes
Cooking time: 8–12 minutes

2 x 150 g (5 oz) sirloin steaks
juice of 2 limes
1 tablespoon honey
1 red chilli, deseeded and finely sliced
3 spring onions, sliced
2 tomatoes, sliced
3 shallots, finely sliced
½ Chinese leaf head, finely sliced
½ cucumber, deseeded and sliced
small handful coriander leaves, roughly torn
small handful basil leaves, roughly torn
1 tablespoon sesame seeds, toasted
freshly ground black pepper

• Heat a griddle until hot, season the steaks on both sides with pepper and cook on the griddle for 4–6 minutes, depending on how pink you like your beef. Leave the steaks to rest for 5 minutes.

• Make the dressing by whisking together the lime juice, honey and chilli.

• Toss together the remaining ingredients. Then slice the steak and add it to the salad with the dressing. Gently toss the salad once again before serving.

ROASTED WINTER VEGETABLE & WATERCRESS SALAD WITH TAHINI DRESSING

Tahini is a paste that is made from crushed sesame seeds – it has a very strong flavour and is a superb way of adding creaminess to sauces and dressings.

SERVES 4

Prep time: 15 minutes
Cooking time: 20–25 minutes

3 parsnips, peeled and cut into bite-
   size pieces
250 g (5 oz) butternut squash, cut into
   bite-size pieces
250 g (3½ oz) Brussels sprouts,
   trimmed and halved
1 red onion, cut into wedges
3 tablespoons olive oil
2 garlic cloves, crushed
2 tablespoons tahini paste
juice of 1 lemon
40 g (1¾ oz) watercress
2 tablespoons toasted walnuts
1 tablespoon chopped chives
freshly ground black pepper

• Preheat the oven to 200°C (400°F), Gas Mark 6.

• Place the vegetables in two roasting trays and sprinkle with the pepper and 2 tablespoons of the olive oil. Roast for 20–25 minutes until the vegetables are tender and starting to caramelize at the edges.

• Meanwhile, make the dressing by whisking together the remaining olive oil, garlic, tahini and lemon juice.

• Scatter the watercress over a large platter and top with the roasted vegetables.

• Pour over the dressing, sprinkle with the walnuts and chives and serve.

JERUSALEM ARTICHOKE SOUP WITH PARSLEY PESTO

The pesto really lifts the flavour of this soup and is well worth the extra effort. Any leftover pesto makes a great dipping sauce for raw vegetables, too.

SERVES 4

Prep time: 20 minutes
Cooking time: 45 minutes

4–5 tablespoons olive oil
625 g (1¼ lb) Jerusalem artichokes, chopped
1 onion, chopped
2 leeks, trimmed and chopped
350 g (11 ½ oz) carrots, chopped
1.2 litres (2 pints) vegetable stock
large bunch parsley
100 g (3½ oz) pine nuts, toasted
1 garlic clove, chopped
freshly ground black pepper

• Heat 1 tablespoon of the oil in a pan and add the artichokes, onion, leeks and carrots, and cook over a low heat to sweat them for about 20 minutes, until soft.

• Add the stock, bring to the boil and then simmer for 20–25 minutes.

• Meanwhile, make the pesto by placing the parsley, pine nuts and garlic in a blender or food processor, and process until broken down (or use a pestle and mortar). Gradually pour in the remaining oil until you have a thin paste. Season to taste with black pepper.

• Liquidize the soup until smooth, then serve with a swirl of pesto on the top.

SPICED PARSNIP & APPLE SOUP

Parsnip and apple is a perfect combination and both ingredients are in season at the same time. Adding a little spice makes this a perfect winter soup.

SERVES 4

Prep time: 10 minutes
Cooking time: 46–55 minutes

1 tablespoon olive oil
1 large onion, chopped
1 garlic clove, finely diced
2.5 cm (1 inch) piece fresh root ginger, finely diced
6 parsnips, chopped
2 teaspoons garam masala
1 litre (1¾ pints) vegetable stock
freshly ground black pepper
fresh chopped coriander, to serve

• Heat the oil in a pan and sauté the onion for 4–5 minutes, until starting to soften.

• Add the garlic, ginger and parsnips and cook for 2–3 minutes before stirring in the garam masala.

• Pour in the stock, bring to the boil, then cover the pan and simmer for 40–45 minutes until the parsnips are really soft.

• Blend the soup with a blender or food processor and season to taste with black pepper.

• Serve the soup sprinkled with chopped coriander.

SAVOY CABBAGE & BACON SOUP

Cabbage is a great tasting vegetable and very good in supporting detoxification.

SERVES 4

Prep time: 8 minutes
Cooking time: 18–22 minutes

1 tablespoon olive oil
2 garlic cloves, chopped
½ teaspoon fennel seeds
2 leeks, trimmed and thinly sliced
2 back bacon rashers, chopped
1 small Savoy cabbage, shredded
1.2 litres (2 pints) vegetable stock
freshly ground black pepper

• Heat the oil in a pan and cook the garlic, fennel seeds and leeks for 2–3 minutes, until starting to soften.

• Add the chopped bacon and continue to cook for 4–5 minutes.

• Add the cabbage and cook, stirring, for 1–2 minutes.

• Pour in the stock, bring to the boil and then simmer for 10–12 minutes.

• Serve the soup as it is, or use a blender or food processor to make it smooth and creamy.

• Season to taste before serving.

LETTUCE, PEA & MINT SOUP

An unusual sounding soup, but try it as it tastes so fresh and the colour is such a beautiful splash of colour at the table.

SERVES 4

Prep time: 8 minutes
Cooking time: 8–18 minutes

1 tablespoon olive oil
2 shallots, sliced
1 large round lettuce, leaves separated
500 g (1 lb) fresh or frozen peas,
    defrosted
1 litre (1¾ pints) vegetable stock
bunch of mint, roughly chopped
freshly ground black pepper
watercress, to garnish

• Heat the oil in a pan and sauté the shallots for 2 minutes.

• Stir in the lettuce and peas and cook for 1 minute before pouring in the stock and the mint.

• Bring to a simmer and cook for 5 minutes (10 minutes if the peas are fresh).

• Process the soup in a blender or food processor until smooth. Then season to taste and serve with a sprig of watercress.

CHILLED AVACODO SOUP WITH RED PEPPER SALSA

This cold, creamy soup is ideal for a warm summer's day. And it is rich in essential fats, too.

SERVES 4

Prep time: 15 minutes, plus chilling
Cooking time: 2–3 minutes

4 large avocados
juice of 1 lime
½ red chilli, deseeded and finely diced
900 ml (1½ pints) vegetable
stock, chilled
freshly ground black pepper
ice cubes, to serve

SALSA

2 tablespoons pumpkin seeds
2 spring onions, finely sliced
½ red pepper, cored, deseeded
and diced
¼ cucumber, diced
1 tablespoon coriander leaves
2 tablespoons olive oil
2 teaspoons lemon juice

• Halve, stone and peel the avocados, then roughly chop the flesh and place in a food processor or blender with the lime juice, chilli and stock. Blend until smooth, then season with pepper and chill for 15 minutes.

• Meanwhile, heat a dry nonstick frying pan over a medium-low heat and dry-fry the pumpkin seeds for 2–3 minutes, shaking the pan occasionally, until golden brown and toasted. Leave to cool.

• To make the salsa, place the toasted pumpkin seeds in a bowl, add the remaining ingredients and mix together.

• Place a couple of ice cubes in each of 4 shallow bowls, then pour over the soup. Spoon over the salsa and serve immediately.

INDIAN TURMERIC SOUP

Turmeric has been used in India for a long time, and is characterized by its distinctive flavour and also by its health properties – it is known to act as a natural anti-inflammatory and antibacterial agent, and is therefore an excellent choice to include in the diet.

SERVES 2

Prep time: 12 minutes
Cooking time: 15 minutes

2 tablespoons olive oil or coconut oil
1 teaspoon cumin seeds
1 teaspoon coriander seeds
1 teaspoon mustard seeds
1 teaspoon ground turmeric
3 cm (1¼ inches) piece fresh root
     ginger, grated
3 spring onions, sliced
2 garlic cloves, sliced
2 small carrots, thinly sliced
½ cauliflower, broken into florets
900 ml (1½ pints) vegetable or chicken
     stock
small handful curry leaves
freshly ground black pepper
coriander sprigs, to serve (optional)

• Heat the oil in a pan and add the spices. Cook for 1 minute then add the ginger, spring onion and garlic and cook for another minute.

• Add the carrots and cauliflower and cook for a minute, stirring to coat the vegetables with all the spices.

• Add the stock and curry leaves, then season with black pepper and bring to a simmer. Cook for 10–12 minutes, until the vegetables are tender.

• Serve in warm bowls with a few sprigs of coriander.

3

FISH

LEMON & GINGER SCALLOPS

This dish gives the classic combination of seafood and lemon an Asian twist with the addition of ginger.

SERVES 3–4

Prep time:10 minutes
Cooking time:10 minutes

2 tablespoons vegetable oil
8 cleaned king scallops, corals removed (optional), cut into thick slices
½ bunch of spring onions, thinly sliced diagonally
½ teaspoon turmeric
3 tablespoons lemon juice
2-cm piece of ginger, peeled and finely sliced
salt and pepper

• Heat a wok until hot. Add 1 tablespoon of the oil and heat over a gentle heat until foaming. Add the sliced scallops and stir-fry for 3 minutes. Remove the wok from the heat. Using a slotted spoon, transfer the scallops to a plate and set aside.

• Return the wok to a medium heat, add the remaining oil and heat until hot. Add the spring onions and turmeric and stir-fry for a few seconds. Add the lemon juice and bring to the boil, then stir in the ginger.

• Return the scallops and their juices to the wok and toss until heated though. Season to taste with salt and pepper and serve immediately.

SKATE WINGS WITH SHRIMPS & CAPERS ON WILTED SPINACH

The term 'skate' is used in Britain to describe almost any member of the ray family of fish. Skate wings are the pectoral fins and are normally served with a caper sauce – this recipe adds delicious brown shrimps for even more flavour.

SERVES 4

Prep time: 10 minutes
Cooking time: 12 minutes

500 g (1 lb) baby spinach leaves, rinsed
4 x 200 g (7 oz) skate wings, skinned
   and trimmed
1½ tablespoons olive oil
2 tablespoons capers
juice of 1 lemon
75 g (3 oz) cooked brown shrimps
1 tablespoon chopped parsley
freshly ground black pepper

• Place the washed spinach in a pan with just the residual water on the leaves and cook over a low heat, covered, until wilted.

• Meanwhile, season the skate wings with black pepper.

• Heat the olive oil in a large frying pan and cook the skate wings in a single layer for 3–4 minutes on each side, until golden. Remove from the pan and keep warm.

• Add the capers, lemon juice, shrimps and parsley to the pan and cook for 1 minute, just to heat through.

• Serve the skate wings on a bed of wilted spinach, with the shrimps and capers spooned over the top.

VIETNAMESE PRAWN SALAD

This salad has a great combination of flavours and textures – there is lots of crunch and heat, alongside the soft prawns and zingy lime!

SERVES 2

Prep time: 20 minutes

1 garlic clove, crushed
½ small red chilli, deseeded and finely diced
juice of 2 limes
½ teaspoon honey
½ teaspoon sesame oil
1 tablespoon olive oil
1 pak choi, chopped
150 g (5 oz) cooked tiger prawns
¼ cucumber, cut into matchsticks
1 carrot, cut into matchsticks
4 spring onions, shredded
small handful of coriander leaves
1 tablespoon cashew nuts, toasted and roughly chopped

• Make the dressing by whisking together the garlic, chilli, lime juice, honey and oils.

• Toss together the remaining ingredients, then toss in the dressing.

• Divide between 2 bowls and serve.

SPINACH-STUFFED SQUID

Squid tubes make perfect pockets for stuffing, and look very impressive too!

SERVES 4

Prep time: 20 minutes
Cooking time: 18 minutes

8 squid tubes and tentacles, cleaned
3 tablespoons olive oil
1 onion, finely diced
1 garlic clove, finely chopped
200 g (7 oz) baby spinach leaves
10 large king prawns, chopped
1 tablespoon pine nuts, toasted
1 egg yolk
freshly ground black pepper
1 tablespoon chopped basil, to serve
juice of 1 lemon, to serve

• Preheat the oven to 180°C (350°F), Gas Mark 4. Remove the tentacles from the squid body by pulling them out and cutting them off and put to one side.

• Heat 1 tablespoon of the olive oil in a frying pan and cook the onion for 4–5 minutes, until softened.

• Stir in the garlic and baby spinach leaves and keep stirring until the leaves have wilted.

• Stir in the chopped prawns, pine nuts and egg yolk and season with black pepper. Cook for 1–2 minutes, then remove from the heat and leave to cool slightly.

• Using a teaspoon, spoon the mixture into the squid tubes – do not overfill as they may split during cooking.

• Heat the remaining olive oil in a frying pan and cook the squid tubes for 5 minutes, basting them with the oil and turning once. Place in a roasting tin and roast in the oven for 2–3 minutes.

• Meanwhile, cook the tentacles in the frying pan for 2 minutes.

• Serve the tubes with the tentacles spooned over the top, sprinkled with chopped basil and lemon juice.

GRILLED OYSTERS

Raw oysters are not to everyone's taste, but if you try them cooked you'll find that they taste quite different. If you don't want to open your own oysters, ask your fishmonger to prepare them for you.

SERVES 4

Cooking time: 7 minutes

3 tablespoons olive oil
2 garlic cloves, finely chopped
juice of ½ lemon
½ teaspoon chilli flakes
½ teaspoon freshly milled black pepper
1 tablespoon finely chopped parsley
16 whole fresh oysters, shucked

• Preheat the grill to hot.

• Heat the oil in a small pan on a gentle heat. Add the garlic and cook for about 30 seconds, just to bring out the fragrance of the garlic. Add the lemon juice, chilli flakes, pepper and parsley, and remove from the heat.

• Place the oysters on a baking tray and cook under the hot grill for 2–3 minutes.

• Spoon over the parsley dressing and cook for a further 2–3 minutes. Serve immediately.

LEMON SOLE WITH RATATOUILLE

While new potatoes and fish go well together, the sole is also good with couscous. Omit the potato from the ratatouille and stir through the couscous.

SERVES 4

Prep time: 8 minutes
Cooking time: 30 minutes

12 small waxy new potatoes, scrubbed
2 tablespoons olive oil
1 yellow pepper, cored, deseeded and
    cut into 1 cm (½ inch) dice
2 small courgettes, halved horizontally,
    then cut into crescents
300 g (10 oz) ripe cherry tomatoes,
    halved
2 spring onions, finely chopped
12 basil leaves
4 whole lemon sole, gutted
1 lemon
salt and pepper

• Cook the potatoes in salted boiling water. Drain, then rinse under cold running water to stop the cooking process and drain again.

• Pour 1 tablespoon of the oil into a frying pan over a high heat, add the yellow pepper and fry for 2 minutes until slightly coloured but still crunchy. Add the courgettes and tomatoes and cook until the tomatoes start to break up. Quarter the potatoes lengthways and add to the rest of the vegetables. Finally, stir in the spring onions and basil leaves. Season to taste with salt and pepper.

• Place the lemon sole on a baking sheet covered in foil. Season the fish with salt and pepper and drizzle with the remaining oil. Place under a preheated grill and cook for 5–6 minutes on each side. Squeeze some lemon juice over each fish. Serve with the warm ratatouille.

GRIDDLED SARDINES WITH GREMOLATA

Sardines are inexpensive but very good for you – rich in omega-3 fats they are the perfect food for the brain. This is a great recipe for a summer barbecue.

SERVES 4

Prep time: 8 minutes
Cooking time: 6–8 minutes

3 lemons
100 g (3½ oz) flat leaf parsley, chopped
1 garlic clove, finely chopped
16–20 sardines, gutted
freshly ground black pepper
1–2 tbsp extra virgin olive oil

• Grate the rind of one of the lemons.

• Make the gremolata by placing the chopped parsley in a bowl with the grated rind and garlic and mix well.

• Season the sardines with pepper.

• Heat a griddle until very hot and cook the sardines for 3–4 minutes on each side, until cooked through (alternatively, cook them on a hot barbecue). Cut the remaining lemons in half and cook them on the griddle alongside the sardines.

• Serve the sardines sprinkled with the parsley gremolata, and a drizzle of olive oil and a griddled lemon half.

RED MULLET AND ROASTED FENNEL

Fennel is the perfect accompaniment to fish and, if you can't find red mullet, this recipe works well with sea bream, too.

SERVES 2

Prep time: 10 minutes, plus standing
Cooking time: 35 minutes

2 fennel bulbs, trimmed and sliced
1 tablespoon olive oil
4 red mullet fillets, about 150–175 g
    (5–6 oz) each

CHILLI OIL
2 garlic cloves, finely chopped
1 teaspoon chilli flakes
75 ml (3 fl oz) olive oil
2 tablespoons chopped parsley

• Preheat the oven to 200°C (400°F), Gas Mark 6.

• To make the chilli oil, place the garlic, chilli flakes and oil in a small saucepan and heat very gently for 5 minutes. Remove from the heat and leave to stand while you cook the fennel.

• Place the fennel in a roasting tin and drizzle with the oil. Place in the preheated oven for 30 minutes until the fennel is tender.

• Towards the end of the cooking time, preheated the grill to hot then cook the fish under the grill for 3–4 minutes on each side, or until the fish is cooked through.

• Stir the parsley into the chilli oil. Spoon the fennel on to 2 warmed plates, top with the fish and serve drizzled with the chilli oil.

PAN-FRIED SEA BASS WITH GAZPACHO SALSA

The flavours in the gazpacho salsa complement the sea bass beautifully. You can make the salsa as spicy as you want with the addition of more red chilli.

SERVES 4

Prep time: 18 minutes
Cooking time: 4–6 minutes

4 tomatoes, diced
1 red pepper, deseeded and diced
3 spring onions, finely sliced
¼ cucumber, diced
1 garlic clove, crushed
½ red chilli, deseeded and finely diced
5-6 basil leaves, shredded
juice of 1 lime
3 tablespoons extra virgin olive oil
4 sea bass fillets
freshly ground black pepper

• Make the salsa by mixing together the tomatoes, red pepper, spring onions, cucumber, garlic, chilli and basil leaves, and then stirring in the lime juice and 1½ tablespoons of the olive oil. Leave this to stand at room temperature to allow the flavours to develop.

• Score the skin of the sea bass fillets, then season with pepper. Heat the remaining oil in a frying pan and cook the fillets skin-side down for 3–4 minutes before turning them over and cooking for a further 1-2 minutes.

• Divide the salsa between four plates and top each one with a sea bass fillet. Pour over any juices from the pan and serve.

GRIDDLED SWORDFISH WITH HERB GREMOLATA

This tasty herb gremolata is perfect served with a 'meaty' firm fish such as swordfish – you can vary the herbs to suit your taste.

SERVES 4

Prep time: 8 minutes
Cooking time: 6–8 minutes

3 tablespoons olive oil
juice of 1 lemon
3 tablespoons chopped mint leaves
1 tablespoon chopped basil leaves
1 garlic clove, crushed
4 x 150 g (5 oz) swordfish steaks
freshly ground black pepper
crisp green salad, to serve

• Whisk together the olive oil, lemon juice, herbs, garlic and pepper to make the gremolata.

• Heat a griddle until hot.

• Brush the swordfish steaks with 2 tablespoons of the gremolata, then cook on the griddle for 3–4 minutes each side until it is cooked through.

• Serve the steaks with the remaining gremolata spooned over the top, accompanied by a crisp green salad.

4

MEAT

FRUIT-STUFFED PORK FILLET WITH ROSEMARY

This is a lovely dish to make on a cold winter's day as it fills the house with lovely aromas. The flavours of peach and rosemary work really well together.

SERVES 4

Prep time: 30 minutes
Cooking time: 1¾–2 hours

2 pork fillets, about 250–300 g (8–10 oz) each
3 tablespoons roughly chopped rosemary leaves
3 tablespoons olive oil
1 onion, finely chopped
2 fresh peaches, stoned and roughly chopped
½ teaspoon ground coriander
pinch of ground cumin
pepper

• Lay the pork fillets on a chopping board and make a cut across the meat lengthways through the centre, about 1.5 cm (¾ inch) away from the other side, and open out. Scatter the rosemary leaves over both the inside and then the outside of the meat pieces and season generously with pepper.

• Heat 2 tablespoons of the oil in a large frying pan and cook the onion over a medium heat, stirring, for 4 minutes until softened. Add the peaches and spices and cook for 1 minute.

• Spoon half the peach mixture down the centre of one of the fillets and the remaining mixture down the centre of the other. Gently press the meat back together and tie with kitchen string in several places to hold the stuffing in place.

• Heat the remaining tablespoon of oil in the cleaned frying pan and cook the pork over a gentle heat, turning frequently, for 20 minutes, covering the pan for the final 5–10 minutes of the cooking time, until cooked through and tender.

• Serve the pork hot, sliced into rounds.

CHICKEN TAGINE

The lengthy cooking time of this dish is well worth the wait. The chicken becomes very tender and the spices infuse the sauce.

SERVES 4

Prep time:20 minutes, plus marinating
Cooking time:1 hour 40 minutes

8 large skinless chicken thighs or
    1 whole chicken, jointed
1 teaspoon ground cumin
1 teaspoon ground coriander
½ teaspoon ground turmeric
1 teaspoon ground ginger
1 teaspoon paprika
3 tablespoons olive oil
2 onions, cut into wedges
2 garlic cloves, finely sliced
1 fennel bulb, sliced
300 g (10 oz) small new potatoes
handful of sultanas
8 ready-to-eat dried apricots
100 g (3½ oz) green olives (optional)
pinch of saffron threads
400 ml (14 fl oz) hot gluten-free
    chicken stock
small bunch of coriander, chopped
salt and black pepper

• Slash each piece of chicken 2–3 times with a small knife. Mix together the spices and half the olive oil, rub over the chicken pieces, cover and marinate in the refrigerator for at least 2 hours, preferably overnight.

• Heat the remaining oil in a tagine or large flameproof casserole, add the chicken pieces and fry for 4–5 minutes until golden all over. Add the onion, garlic and fennel to the pan and continue to fry for 2–3 minutes.

• Add all the remaining ingredients, except the coriander, and stir well. Cover and simmer for about 1½ hours or until the chicken begins to fall off the bone. Season well and stir in the coriander.

PAN-FRIED GAMMON STEAKS WITH PINEAPPLE SALSA

To prevent the gammon steaks from curling as they cook, snip the fat at intervals before cooking.

SERVES 2

Prep time: 15 minutes
Cooking time: 10–14 minutes

¼ small pineapple, 'eyes' removed, cored and diced
½ small red onion, finely diced
½ green pepper, deseeded and diced
¼ teaspoon smoked paprika
1½ tablespoons olive oil
2 x 200 g (7 oz) thick cut gammon steaks
freshly ground black pepper
crisp green salad, to serve

• Mix together the pineapple, onion, pepper, paprika and ½ tablespoon of the olive oil for the salsa. Add black pepper to taste. Leave to stand at room temperature.

• Heat the remaining olive oil in a pan. Snip the fat of the gammon at 2.5 cm (1 inch) intervals to prevent the steaks from curling up while cooking. Cook the gammon steaks for 5–7 minutes each side, until golden.

• Serve the gammon steaks with the pineapple salsa and a crisp green salad.

ROAST CHICKEN WITH FENNEL & LEMON

Fennel and lemon give chicken such a fresh, tangy flavour. Always aim to buy good-quality, organic chicken.

SERVES 4

Prep time: 8 minutes
Cooking time: 38–45 minutes

2 tablespoons olive oil
8 chicken thighs
2 large fennel bulbs, halved and sliced
4 garlic cloves, crushed
grated rind and juice of 1 lemon
freshly ground black pepper
vegetables, to serve

• Preheat the oven to 200°C (400°F), Gas Mark 6.

• Heat the oil in a frying pan and cook the chicken for 8–10 minutes, browning it all over.

• Transfer to a roasting tin and toss with the fennel, garlic, lemon rind and juice and black pepper.

• Roast for 30–35 minutes, until the chicken is cooked and the fennel is starting to brown around the edges.

• Serve with vegetables of your choice.

LEEK & CHESTNUT STUFFED BREAST OF LAMB

Stuffing a breast of lamb not only makes the meat go further, but also adds great flavour.

SERVES 4

Prep time: 20 minutes
Cooking time: see recipe

1 x 750 g (1½ lb) breast of lamb, boned
2 teaspoons fennel seeds
1 tablespoon olive oil
2 leeks, trimmed and finely chopped
2 garlic cloves, finely chopped
175 g (6 oz) cooked, peeled chestnuts, finely chopped
1 tablespoon chopped parsley
½ tablespoon chopped rosemary
freshly ground black pepper
steamed vegetables, to serve

• Preheat the oven to 180°C (350°F), Gas Mark 4.

• Place the breast of lamb on a board and unroll. Season on both sides with the black pepper and fennel seeds.

• Heat the oil in a frying pan and cook the leeks and garlic for 4–5 minutes, then remove from the heat. Stir the remaining ingredients into the pan, then leave to cool slightly.

• Spread the stuffing evenly over the surface of the lamb breast and re-roll, securing with kitchen string at 2–3 cm (1–1½ inch) intervals along the joint.

• Weigh the joint with the stuffing, place in a roasting tin and cook for 25 minutes per 450 g (14½ oz) plus 25 minutes for medium-cooked lamb, or 30 minutes per 450 g (14½ oz) plus 30 minutes for well-done lamb.

• Serve with steamed vegetables.

TURKEY KOFTAS WITH CRUNCHY SALAD

These spicy little koftas can be made in advance and then cooked over a summer barbecue.

SERVES 4

Prep time: 28 minutes
Cooking time: 6–8 minutes

500 g (1 lb) turkey mince
1 red onion, finely diced
1 tablespoon harissa paste
1 teaspoon cumin seeds
1 garlic clove, crushed
2 apples, cored and thinly sliced
6 radishes, thinly sliced
1 cucumber, cut into matchsticks
2 carrots, grated
1 tablespoon chopped mint
1 tablespoon extra virgin olive oil
2 tablespoon sesame seeds, toasted
2 limes, to serve

• Preheat the grill to hot.

• Mix together the turkey mince, onion, harissa, cumin seeds and garlic and shape into 8 small oval koftas. Thread each one onto a small metal skewer.

• Mix together the apples, radishes, cucumber, carrots, mint, olive oil and sesame seeds.

• Cook the koftas under the hot grill for 6–8 minutes, turning occasionally, until cooked through.

• Serve the koftas with the crunchy salad and a squeeze of lime juice.

LEMONY POACHED CHICKEN

Poaching the chicken makes the meat very tender and allows the flesh to absorb all the flavours in the liquid.

SERVES 4

Prep time: 10 minutes
Cooking time: 1¾–2 hours

1 whole free-range chicken, about
   1.5–2 kg (3–4 lb)
3 shallots, halved
2 garlic cloves, lightly crushed
1 celery stick, roughly chopped
1 rosemary sprig
8 black peppercorns
100 ml (3½ fl oz) balsamic vinegar
1 preserved lemon, chopped
1 small bunch of sage, leaves removed
2 tablespoons extra virgin rapeseed oil
salt and pepper

• Place the chicken, shallots, garlic, celery, rosemary and black peppercorns in a large saucepan. Add the balsamic vinegar and pour in enough cold water to almost cover the chicken. Place over a medium heat and bring slowly to the boil, skimming the surface to remove any scummy froth. Cover and simmer gently for 1 hour.

• Add the preserved lemon and half the sage leaves, then simmer gently for a further 15–30 minutes, depending on the size of the chicken, until the juices run clear when the thickest part of the leg is pierced with a knife. Carefully remove from the pan and place in a deep dish, cover with foil and leave to rest. Increase the heat and boil the stock for 20–25 minutes or until reduced by half. Remove from the heat and leave to cool slightly. Season to taste.

• Heat the oil in a small frying pan and shallow-fry the remaining sage leaves for 30 seconds until crisp. Remove with a slotted spoon and drain on kitchen paper.

• Cut the chicken meat from the carcass, discarding the skin, and spoon into shallow bowls with plenty of cooking broth. Garnish with the crisp sage leaves and serve with steamed asparagus and broccoli.

SLOW-ROASTED PORK BELLY WITH CELERIAC MASH

Pork belly is best cooked slowly, and is well worth the wait. It is also just as good when it's cold – if there is any left!

SERVES 4

Prep time: 15 minutes
Cooking time: 2½ hours

1½ kg (3 lb) pork belly, skin scored
3 rosemary sprigs, leaves stripped
10 black peppercorns
750 g (1½ lb) celeriac, chopped
2 pears, cored and chopped
2 tablespoons olive oil
2 onions, sliced
1 tablespoon thyme leaves, roughly
    chopped

• Preheat the oven to 220°C (425°F), Gas Mark 7.

• Pat the skin of the pork dry with kitchen paper.

• Place the rosemary leaves and pepper into a small blender or food processor and blitz until broken down together (or use a pestle and mortar).

• Rub the spice mix over the skin of the pork, working it into the cuts in the skin. Place in a roasting tin and roast for 30 minutes.

• Reduce the oven temperature to 170°C (325°F), Gas Mark 3 and continue to cook for 1½ hours. For the last 20 minutes of cooking, increase the oven temperature back up to 220°C (425°F), Gas Mark 7.

• When the pork is almost cooked, place the celeriac in a pan of water and bring to the boil, then simmer for 20 minutes, adding the chopped pears for the last 5 minutes of cooking, until the celeriac is tender. Mash until smooth.

• Meanwhile, heat the oil in a frying pan and cook the onion for 15–18 minutes until soft and starting to caramelize. Stir in the thyme leaves towards the end of the cooking time.

• Let the pork rest for 10 minutes before carving it into thick strips and serving with a big spoonful of mash and caramelized onions.

MORROCAN RACK OF LAMB

This is quite a spicy dish; if you want to make it milder just use less chilli powder. Be sure to ask your butcher to trim the excess fat off the rack of lamb.

SERVES 2

Preparation time 10 minutes, plus resting
Cooking time 15–25 minutes

2 tablespoons olive oil
½ teaspoon ground cumin
½ teaspoon chilli powder
¼ teaspoon turmeric
¼ teaspoon paprika
¼ teaspoon ground coriander
2 garlic cloves, crushed
3 tablespoons chopped parsley
juice of ½ lemon
6-cutlet rack of lamb
steamed kale, to serve

• Preheat the oven to 200°C (400°F), Gas Mark 6.

• Mix together the oil, all the spices, garlic, parsley and lemon juice in a bowl. Place the rack of lamb in a roasting tin and spread the spice mixture over the top.

• Roast in the preheated oven for 15–25 minutes, depending on how rare you like your lamb. Leave to rest for 5–6 minutes.

• Serve with steamed kale.

VENISON STEAK WITH WILD MUSHROOMS & SWEET RED ONIONS

Venison has the benefit of being fuller in flavour than beef and slightly leaner. Use any wild mushrooms that are in season.

SERVES 2

Prep time: 14 minutes
Cooking time: 25 minutes

2 tablespoons olive oil
2 red onions, sliced
2 sprigs thyme
2 teaspoons honey
2 x 150 g (5 oz) venison steaks
100 g (3½ oz) wild mushrooms (such as chanterelles or girolles)
freshly ground black pepper
steamed greens, to serve

• Heat 1 tablespoon of olive oil in a pan and cook the onions over a medium heat for 5-6 minutes, stirring occasionally.

• Add the thyme with honey, and continue to cook for 8-10 minutes, until the onions start to caramelize.

• Heat a griddle until hot and cook the venison steaks for 4-5 minutes on each side, depending on how pink you like your steak.

• Meanwhile, heat the remaining oil in a frying pan and cook the wild mushrooms, seasoning them with black pepper.

• Serve the venison scattered with the wild mushrooms, with the sweet red onions and the steamed greens on the side.

5

VEGETARIAN

SWEET POTATO BUBBLE & SQUEAK

This dish works well for breakfast or brunch, and allows you to use up any leftover vegetables – a reliable combination is cabbage, Brussels sprouts, leeks and fennel, but don't be afraid to try your own combinations.

SERVES 2

Prep time: 15 minutes
Cooking time: 15–20 minutes

2 sweet potatoes, chopped
1 tablespoon olive oil
1 onion, sliced
200 g (7 oz) Brussels sprouts, shredded
2 eggs
1 tablespoon chopped chives
freshly ground black pepper

• Cook the sweet potato in a pan of simmering water for 8-10 minutes, until softened.

• Meanwhile, heat the oil in a frying pan and cook the onion for 5-6 minutes. Then add the sprouts and continue to cook, stirring occasionally, for 3-4 minutes.

• Once the potatoes are cooked, drain and then return them to the pan and mash them roughly. Add to the Brussels sprouts mixture and mix well.

• Poach the eggs in a frying pan of simmering water for 5-6 minutes, or until cooked to your liking.

• Divide the bubble and squeak between two plates and top each one with a poached egg. Sprinkle with chives and pepper before serving.

BRAISED CELERY HEARTS

This alternative way of preparing celery makes a nice change from serving it as a cold salad ingredient.

SERVES 2

Prep time: 10 minutes
Cooking time: 1 hour 10 minutes

2 celery hearts
2 bay leaves
150 ml (¼ pint) vegetable stock
grated rind and juice of 1 orange
50 g (2 oz) walnut halves
freshly ground black pepper

• Preheat the oven to 180°C (350°F), Gas Mark 4.

• Trim the celery stalks and cut into quarters lengthways. Place in an ovenproof dish.

• Season the celery with pepper, then add the bay leaves, stock, orange rind and juice and sprinkle over the walnut halves.

• Cover the dish with foil and then cook for 1 hour. Remove the foil, check how tender the celery is and, if needed, cook uncovered for a further 10 minutes.

SUMMER FRITTATA

This protein-rich meal can be served for breakfast, brunch or lunch. It could also be made to take on a picnic or to work in a lunch box.

SERVES 4

Prep time: 16 minutes
Cooking time: 34–40 minutes

350 g (11½ oz) sweet potato, peeled
   and chopped into bite-size pieces
2 tablespoons olive oil
1 red onion, chopped
1 red pepper, deseeded and sliced
125 g (4 oz) fresh or frozen peas
7 medium eggs
1 tablespoon chopped mint
1 tablespoon snipped chives
freshly ground black pepper, to serve

• Cook the sweet potato in a pan of boiling water for 8 minutes until just tender. Drain.

• Heat half the oil in a frying pan and cook the onion with the sweet potato and red peppers for 5–6 minutes. Add the peas and cook for one minute more.

• Beat the eggs in a large bowl, pour in the vegetables and mix well. Season and stir in the herbs.

• Heat the remaining oil in the same frying pan and pour the egg and vegetables back into the pan.

• Cook over a low heat for 15–18 minutes, until the bottom of the frittata is golden. Meanwhile, preheat the grill to hot.

• Finish cooking under the grill for 6–8 minutes, until golden on top.

• Leave the frittata to stand for a minute, then run a knife around the edge of the pan, place a plate or board on top and turn over to remove from the pan.

• Cut into wedges to serve hot or cold.

ROASTED RED & YELLOW PEPPERS

Roasted peppers are extremely versatile. You can fill them with vegetables, or roast them with garlic and leave them to cool, then slice and serve in a salad.

SERVES 4

Preparation time 10 minutes
Cooking time 25 minutes

2 red peppers, halved, cored and
   deseeded
2 yellow peppers, halved, cored and
   deseeded
1 red onion, cut into 8 wedges
18 cherry tomatoes
2 courgettes, halved and sliced
3 garlic cloves, sliced
2 tablespoons extra-virgin olive oil
1 teaspoon cumin seeds
2 tablespoons flaked almonds
freshly ground black pepper
crisp green salad, to serve

• Preheat the oven to 200°C (400°F), Gas Mark 6.

• Place the pepper halves, cut side up, in a roasting tin and divide the remaining vegetables and garlic among them.

• Sprinkle with the oil, cumin seeds and flaked almonds and season with pepper.

• Roast in the preheated oven for 25 minutes until tender. Serve with a crisp green salad.

MUSHROOM RAGOUT WITH SWEET POTATO & PARSNIP MASH

This is a really comforting autumnal dish that is at its best when the wild mushrooms are in season – vary the mushrooms you use for a completely different flavour.

SERVES 4

Prep time: 12 minutes
Cooking time: 25 minutes

3 medium parsnips, chopped
3 medium sweet potatoes, chopped
2 tablespoons olive oil
650 g (1 ⅓ lb) mushrooms of your choice, halved or quartered if they are large
1 garlic clove, peeled and finely chopped
1 tablespoon thyme leaves, chopped
250 ml (8 fl oz) vegetable stock
freshly ground black pepper
pinch of nutmeg

• Cook the parsnips and sweet potatoes in a pan of boiling water for 15–18 minutes, until tender.

• Meanwhile, heat the olive oil in a large frying pan and cook the mushrooms and garlic until the mushrooms release their juices, then turn up the heat and cook for a few minutes more to reduce the juices.

• Add the thyme and stock and simmer for about 15 minutes, until the liquid has reduced by about half.

• Drain the parsnips and sweet potatoes and mash with the black pepper and nutmeg.

• Divide the mash between four warmed bowls and spoon over the mushroom ragout.

AUBERGINE, GREEN BEAN & CASHEW CURRY

Making your own curry paste allows you to vary the flavour of a curry but, more importantly, it means you can control the heat. So if you like a really hot curry, then add a few more chillies to this recipe.

SERVES 4

Prep time: 18 minutes
Cooking time: 45 minutes

1 onion, chopped
2 garlic cloves, chopped
2.5 cm (1 inch) piece fresh root ginger, chopped
1 lemon grass stalk, chopped
2 green chillies, deseeded and chopped
½ teaspoon ground cumin
½ teaspoon ground coriander
¼ teaspoon turmeric
3 tablespoons olive oil
3 large aubergines, cut into wedges
200 ml (7 fl oz) passata
1 x 400 ml (14 fl oz) can coconut milk
200 g (7 oz) green beans, trimmed
small bunch coriander, chopped
75 g (3 oz) cashew nuts, toasted

• Place the onion, garlic, ginger, lemon grass, chillies, and spices into a blender or food processor and blend until you have a coarse paste.

• Heat 2 tablespoons of the olive oil in a frying pan and cook the aubergine wedges in batches until lightly golden. Drain on kitchen paper.

• Heat the remaining olive oil in a large pan, add the curry paste and cook for 3-4 minutes, stirring constantly. Add the aubegines and continue to cook for 2–3 minutes.

• Add the passata and coconut milk, bring to a simmer and then add the beans and simmer for 15–18 minutes, covered.

• Stir in the chopped coriander and cashew nuts and serve.

SRI LANKAN EGG CURRY WITH COCONUT SAMBAL

The Sri Lankans normally deep-fry their eggs after boiling them to help them absorb the flavour, but this recipe keeps it simple, and a little healthier! This is delicious served with coconut-flavoured cabbage.

SERVES 4

Prep time: 5 minutes
Cooking time: 16–18 minutes

SAMBAL
½ fresh coconut, flesh only, grated
½–1 teaspoon chilli powder
1 shallot, finely diced
juice of ½ lime
freshly ground black pepper

CURRY
8 eggs
1 tablespoon olive oil
1 teaspoon cumin seeds
¼ teaspoon dill seeds
3 cm (1¼ inch) piece cinnamon stick
1 teaspoon chilli powder
½ teaspoon ground turmeric
1 or 2 small green chillies, chopped
1 onion, chopped
small handful curry leaves
1 x 400 ml (14 fl oz) can coconut milk

• Make the sambal by mixing together the grated coconut flesh and chilli powder until the coconut turns orange. Add the shallot and lime juice and mix well. Season with black pepper.

• Cook the eggs in boiling water for 5 minutes, and then plunge them into cold water before removing the shells.

• Heat the olive oil in a pan and add the spices, chillies and onions and cook for 2 minutes before adding the curry leaves and coconut milk.

• Simmer over a medium heat for 8 minutes, until the sauce starts to thicken.

• Halve the eggs and gently add them to the curry. Cook for 1–2 minutes to heat through the eggs before serving with the spicy sambal.

6
DRINKS AND SNACKS

BUTTERNUT & WALNUT DIP

This dip is a great served with vegetable crudités. It can also be made with pumpkin instead of butternut.

SERVES 4

Prep time: 8 minutes
Cooking time: 20–25 minutes

500 g (1 lb) butternut squash, chopped
2 tablespoons olive oil
½ teaspoon cumin seeds
½ teaspoon smoked paprika
50 g (2 oz) walnuts, toasted
1 tablespoon freshly chopped coriander
vegetable crudités, to serve

• Preheat the oven to 200°C (400°F), Gas Mark 6.

• Place the butternut squash in a roasting tin and toss with the oil, cumin seeds and paprika. Roast for 20–25 minutes until tender. Leave to cool for 10 minutes.

• Process the walnuts in a food processor until roughly chopped, then add the butternut squash, cumin seeds and oil from the pan, along with the chopped coriander. Process until combined, adding a little more oil, if liked, to loosen.

• Serve with vegetable crudités for dipping.

ROOT VEGETABLE CRISPS

Most people love crisps but they are something of a guilty pleasure. These vegetable crisps are just a little bit less naughty.

SERVES 4

Prep time: 15 minutes
Cooking time: 20–30 minutes

3 parsnips
2 beetroot
2 sweet potatoes
1 large carrot
2 tablespoons olive oil
½ teaspoon chilli powder
½ teaspoon freshly ground black
   pepper

• Preheat the oven to 180°C (350°F), Gas Mark 4.

• Thinly slice all the vegetables on the diagonal using a mandolin. Spread the slices on kitchen paper to remove any moisture.

• Place the slices in a large bowl and toss with the oil, chilli powder and black pepper.

• Spread the slices out on baking trays in a single layer.

• Roast in the oven for 20–30 minutes, turning the vegetables over halfway through the cooking time and keeping an eye on them throughout. They are ready when the parsnips are golden brown.

• Spread on kitchen paper again until cool and crisp.

PEA & MINT FRITTERS

As an alternative, you can make these fritters with sweetcorn in place of the peas, or a mixture of both.

MAKES 12–14

Prep time: 12 minutes
Cooking time: 20–25 minutes

250 g (8 oz) sweet potato, chopped
200 g (7 oz) ground almonds
½ tsp baking powder
3 eggs, beaten
200 ml (7 fl oz) non-dairy milk
175 g (6 oz) frozen peas, defrosted
2 tablespoons chopped mint
2 tablespoons olive oil

• Cook the sweet potatoes in a pan of boiling water until tender. Drain and mash the potatoes, then transfer them to a bowl and leave to cool slightly.

• Stir in the ground almonds and baking powder. Then, with a fork, beat in the eggs and milk to give a thick batter. Finally, stir in the peas and mint.

• Heat ½ tablespoon olive oil in a frying pan and add enough tablespoonfuls of the mixture to make 3–4 pancakes. Cook for 3–4 minutes until golden, then carefully flip over and cook for another 2–3 minutes.

• Remove from the pan, keep warm and cook the remaining batter in the same way.

DEVILLED CASHEWS

This is a great snack or pre-dinner nibble. You can make them as spicy or mild as you like, by adding more or less chilli powder.

SERVES 4

Prep time: 4 minutes
Cooking time: 3–4 minutes

4 tablespoons olive oil
2 shallots, thinly sliced
200 g (7 oz) cashew nuts
small handful curry leaves
½ tsp chilli powder
½ 1 teaspoon freshly ground black
    pepper

• Heat the oil in a heavy-based pan until very hot.

• Add the shallots and nuts and fry until golden.

• Add the curry leaves and cook until crisp.

• Remove the shallots, nuts and leaves from the pan with a slotted spoon and place on kitchen paper to drain.

• Mix together the chilli powder and black pepper, then toss the nuts in the mixture to coat well. Leave to cool before serving.

...DE FISH FINGERS

love fish fingers, and they are a guaranteed success with children. This recipe allows you to eat them on the Paleo diet too. Serve as a snack on their own, or with salad as a light lunch.

SERVES 4

Prep time: 15 minutes
Cooking time: 20–22 minutes

60 g (2¼ oz) ground almonds
½ teaspoon paprika
¼ teaspoon freshly ground black
   pepper
600 g (1⅛ lb) cod loin, cut into 'fingers'
crisp green salad, to serve

• Preheat the oven to 180°C (350°F), Gas Mark 4. Line a baking sheet with greaseproof paper.

• Mix together the almonds, paprika and pepper and place in a shallow dish.

• Toss the pieces of fish in the crumbs until coated and place on the baking sheet.

• Cook in the oven for 20–22 minutes, until golden.

SAFFRON AÏOLI WITH VEGETABLE CRUDITÉS

If you like garlic, this is the perfect dip for you — creamy and rich, and perfect eated with a selection of chopped vegetable crudités for a quick snack or pre-dinner nibbles.

SERVES 4

Prep time: 5 minutes

small pinch saffron strands
4 garlic cloves, crushed
3 egg yolks
large pinch freshly ground black
   pepper
juice of ½ lemon
250–300 ml (8 fl oz–½ pint) extra virgin
   olive oil
chopped vegetables, to serve

• Place the saffron in a small bowl, pour over 1 tablespoon boiling water and leave to stand.

• Place the garlic, egg yolks, pepper and lemon juice into a blender or food processor and blend into a paste.

• With the blender or food processor still running, slowly add the olive oil until you have the consistency you like.

• Stir in the water and saffron and serve with chopped vegetables.

SPICED EGGNOG

Eggnog is a sumptuous North American Christmas drink, normally laced with thick cream and dark rum. This version uses non-dairy milk and spices – it is not as rich as the original version, but just as tasty.

SERVES 1

Prep time: 10 minutes
Cooking time: 5 minutes

Prep time: 10 minutes
Cooking time: 5 minutes

1 egg, separated
½ tablespoon honey
200ml (7 fl oz) non-dairy milk
½ vanilla pod
large pinch ground cinnamon
grated nutmeg, to serve

• Whisk together the egg yolk and honey, and in another bowl whisk the egg white until it forms soft peaks.

• Heat the milk with the vanilla pod and cinnamon until it has just come up to a simmer.

• Pour the milk into the egg yolk and honey, whisking continuously, then return to the pan with the egg white and stir until hot.

• Pour into a glass and serve sprinkled with the nutmeg.

OYSTER VIRGIN MARY

This is a twist on a Bloody Mary – but it contains no alcohol. In its place, there is the addition of freshly grated horseradish and an oyster, which gives the drink a real kick.

SERVES 2

Prep time: 5 minutes

3 celery stalks
½ teaspoon grated horseradish
juice of 1 lime
500 ml (17 fl oz) tomato juice
2 oysters, shucked
freshly ground black pepper

• Chop one of the stalks of celery and place in a small blender or food processor with the horseradish and blend with the lime juice until smooth.

• Pour the mixture into a large jug and top up with the tomato juice. Mix well.

• Place the remaining celery stalks in two tall glasses and add an oyster to each one, along with a few ice cubes.

• Pour the Virgin Mary over the ice and sprinkle with black pepper before serving.

RAW COCAO HOT CHOCOLATE

Cocao nibs are pieces of cacao bean that have been roasted and hulled. They have a bitter but strong chocolate flavour (although will not melt down like chocolate), and are perfect for the Paleo diet if you can't give up chocolate. They can be bought in good health food shops, or online.

SERVES 1

Prep time: 1 minute
Cooking time: 5–10 minutes

60 g (2¼ oz) cocao nibs
1 teaspoon ground chia seeds
250 ml (8 fl oz) non-dairy milk
1–2 tsp honey
large pinch of cinnamon powder
cinnamon stick, to serve

• Grind the cocao nibs finely in a coffee grinder.

• Place all the ingredients into a small pan and bring to the boil, stirring occasionally.

• Simmer for 3–4 minutes, until the hot chocolate starts to thicken slightly.

• Strain through a sieve, and then pour into a cup; serve with a cinnamon stick for stirring.

SPICE TEA

Indian spiced tea (chai) is normally made with real tea and served with milk, but this version is a pure combination of spices and lemon. If you wish to make it sweet, just add a little honey.

SERVES 1

Prep time: 4 minutes

3 cardamom pods
1 star anise
3 cloves
2–3 thin slices fresh root ginger
1 cinnamon stick
1 slice of lemon, to serve
honey to taste (optional)

• Lightly crush the cardamom pods then place them in a tall glass with the remaining spices.

• Pour in boiling water and leave to 'brew' for 2–3 minutes.

• Strain the tea or leave the spices in when you serve it, topped with a slice of lemon, and sweetened with honey if you wish.

TROPICAL FRUIT SMOOTHIE

This is a great drink for summer. Look for a really ripe mango so that its flavour is at its best. Tropical fruits have a high sugar content so save them for a special treat.

SERVES 4

Prep time: 10 minutes

1 mango, peeled, stoned
   and chopped
2 kiwifruits, peeled and chopped
1 banana, cut into chunks
425 g (14 oz) can pineapple chunks or
   pieces in natural juice
450 ml (¾ pint) orange or apple juice
handful of ice cubes

• Place all the ingredients in a food processor or blender and blitz until smooth.

• Pour into 4 glasses and serve immediately.

BANANA, RASPBERRY & CHIA SMOOTHIE

Chia seeds are a great source of omega-3 fats and fibre, so are perfect for including in your paleo diet.

SERVES 1

Prep time: 4 minutes

1 banana, chopped
75 g (3 oz) raspberries
2 teaspoons ground chia seeds
300 ml (½ pint) non-dairy milk

• Place all the ingredients into a blender or food processor and blend until smooth.

GREEN SMOOTHIE

This smoothie is a real health boost – add any greens you love and think of it as a summer savoury drink.

SERVES 1

Prep time: 5 minutes

1 apple
1 celery stick
¼ cucumber, chopped
½ teaspoon grated fresh root ginger
small handful of parsley leaves
1 small garlic clove
juice of ½ lemon
300 ml (½ pint) mineral water
freshly ground black pepper
ice cubes, to serve

• Place all the ingredients in a blender and season with pepper, then blend until smooth.

• Pour over ice cubes in a glass and serve immediately.

HONEY NUT SMOOTHIE

This is a really creamy and comforting drink – combine it with your favourite nuts to nibble on as you enjoy it.

SERVES 1

Prep time: 5 minutes

1 banana, chopped
50 g (2 oz) hazelnuts or almonds
300 ml (½ pint) non-dairy milk
2 teaspoons honey
pinch of ground cinnamon

• Place all the ingredients apart from the cinnamon in a blender or food processor and blend until smooth.

• Pour into a long glass over ice, if wished, and sprinkle with a little ground cinnamon.

HOMEMADE LEMONADE

This is such a zingy, lively drink – it is a delectable refreshment for a sunny day, and can also be taken as an immune-supporting drink because it is rich in Vitamin C.

SERVES 2

Prep time: 8 minutes

2 lemons
3 teaspoons honey
sprigs of mint, to serve

• Cut the lemons in half and place them in blender or food processor with 2 teaspoons of the honey and 400 ml (14 fl oz) water. Process until the lemon is completely broken down.

• Pour the mixture through a sieve into a jug. Keep the liquid and return the lemon pulp to the food processor and add the remaining honey and another 200 ml (7 fl oz) water and process again until broken down further.

• Pour the mixture through a sieve into the jug and stir well.

• Pour into ice-filled glasses to serve, with a sprig of mint.

STRAWBERRY FIG SMOOTHIE

Figs are an ideal fruit to use as a smoothie base because their flavour is not too strong, but they add substance and lots of great vitamins and minerals. If your smoothie maker is designed to take them, add the whole fruits (with any green strawberry tops included) – this will give additional fibre.

SERVES 4

Prep time: 5 minutes

3 figs, halved
100 g (3½ oz) strawberries
small handful blanched almonds
pinch of cinnamon
1.2 litres (2 pints) non-dairy milk

• Place all the ingredients into a bender and blend until smooth.

• Serve the smoothie immediately.

7

SWEET THINGS

SUMMER BERRY & CHIA MOUSSE

Chia seeds are rich in omega-3 fats, fibre and antioxidants, so are great seeds for this diet. They are also an effective thickener because they make a gel-like substance when added to liquid.

SERVES 2

Prep time: 5 minutes

100 g (3½ oz) strawberries
100 g (3½ oz) raspberries
100 g (3½ oz) blueberries
100 g (3½ oz) blackberries
1½ teaspoons chia seeds

• Place the fruit and chia seeds into a blender or food processor and blend until smooth.

• Spoon into two bowls or glasses and chill for at least 15 minutes before serving.

COCONUT & BANANA PANCAKES

These sweet pancakes are quick and easy to make and while they do make the perfect pudding, they are delicious as a mid-morning snack.

SERVES 2

Prep time: 5 minutes
Cooking time: 7–8 minutes

2 bananas
45 g (1¾ oz) ground almonds
15 g (½ oz) desiccated coconut
1 egg, beaten
1–2 tablespoons non-dairy milk
1 tablespoon olive oil
1 tablespoon chopped pecan nuts
1 tablespoon honey

• Mash one of the bananas in a bowl and stir in the almonds and coconut.

• Beat in the egg and enough milk to make a thick batter.

• Heat the oil in a large frying pan and spoon four spoonfuls of the batter into the pan.

• Cook for 3–4 minutes until golden underneath and then flip over and cook for a further 3–4 minutes on the other side.

• Slice the remaining banana and serve on top of the pancakes, sprinkled with the chopped pecans and a drizzle of honey.

BLUEBERRY & RASPBERRY COBBLER

This quick and simple pudding could also be made with mango and banana or other soft fruits. Adding the almond, coconut and lemon topping makes it look a little like a traditional cobbler – allow spaces between the topping for the fruit to be seen.

SERVES 4

Prep time: 6 minutes
Cooking time: 12–14 minutes

250 g (8 oz) blueberries
150 g (5 oz) raspberries
140 g (4¾ oz) ground almonds
20 g (¾ oz) desiccated coconut
grated rind of 1 lemon
50 g (2 oz) coconut oil
1 tablespoon honey

• Preheat the oven to 180°C (350°F), Gas Mark 5.

• Place the blueberries and raspberries in an ovenproof dish.

• Mix together the ground almonds, desiccated coconut and lemon rind.

• Melt together the coconut oil and honey, then pour this mixture into the dry ingredients and mix together.

• Spoon the coconut mixture over the fruit and bake for 12–14 minutes, until golden.

COCONUT & MANGO ICE CREAM

It's hard to believe this is dairy-free, because it is so creamy and delicious!

SERVES 4

Prep time: 20 minutes, plus chilling
   time
Cooking time: 8 minutes

1 x 400 ml (14 fl oz) can coconut milk
2 egg yolks
1½ tablespoons honey
30 g (1¼ oz) desiccated coconut
1 mango, diced

• Pour the coconut milk into a pan and bring to a simmer.

• Meanwhile, whisk together the egg yolks and honey in a bowl.

• Whisk the warmed coconut milk into the egg mixture and then return to the pan with the desiccated coconut, and cook for 5 minutes over a medium heat, stirring constantly.

• Pour back into the bowl and leave to cool.

• Stir in the diced mango, and then churn the mixture in an ice-cream maker until frozen. Alternatively, pour the mixture into a freezer-proof container and freeze. Remove the ice cream from the freezer every 45 minutes for 3 hours, whisking it with a fork to break up the ice crystals.

TROPICAL FRUIT SALAD

Tropical fruits are very high in sugar so should not be eaten too often, but this fruit salad is bursting with flavour and makes a great dinner party treat.

SERVES 6

Prep time: 30 minutes

12 lychees, peeled and stoned
1 small pineapple, cut into bite-size pieces, eyes removed
2 mangoes, stoned and cut into bite-size pieces
1 pomegranate, seeds removed
5 passion fruit, flesh only
6 dates, stoned and chopped
1 tablespoon chopped mint
½ tablespoon chopped coriander
large pinch freshly grated nutmeg

• Place all the ingredients together in a large bowl and mix well.

• Leave to stand for at least 10 minutes at room temperature to allow the flavours develop before serving.

RHUBARB & STRAWBERRIES

These fruits are a great summer combination.

SERVES 4

Prep time: 20 minutes
Cooking time: 5 minutes

400 g (13 oz) rhubarb, cut into chunks
1½–2 tablespoons honey
350 g (11½ oz) strawberries, halved

• Place the rhubarb in a pan with 1½ tablespoons water and the honey.

• Bring to a simmer, cover the pan and simmer for 2 minutes.

• Remove from the heat and leave to stand, covered, for 10 minutes.

• Stir in the strawberries. Cover and leave to stand for a further 5 minutes before serving.

COCONUT SHORTBREAD

Coconut oil and flour are useful ingredients in many recipes using this diet; for this shortbread there are only two other ingredients.

MAKES 9 SQUARES

Prep time: 6 minutes
Cooking time: 10–12 minutes

175g (6 oz) coconut flour
50 g (2 oz) ground chia seeds
100 g (3½ oz) coconut oil
4 tablespoons honey

• Preheat the oven to 180°C (350°F), Gas Mark 4. Lightly oil the base of an 18cm (7 inch) square tin.

• Mix together the flour and ground chia seeds in a bowl.

• Melt the coconut oil and honey together, pour them into the dry ingredients and mix well.

• Pour the mixture into the prepared tin and level the top. Bake for 10–12 minutes, until golden on the top.

• Remove the shortbread from the oven, cut into squares and place on a wire rack to cool.

SPICED PLUM COMPÔTE

This compôte is delicious served on its own, or serve it with the shortbread on page 132 – this is a perfect combination for dunking!

SERVES 4

Prep time: 10 minutes
Cooking time: 23–28 minutes

3 tablespoons honey
750 g (1½ lb) ripe plums, halved and
    pitted
2 cinnamon sticks
4 star anise

• Place the honey in a pan with 300 ml (½ pint) water, bring to the boil and let the liquid bubble for 1 minute.

• Add the plums, cinnamon sticks and star anise and simmer for 10–12 minutes.

• Remove the plums from the liquid, then simmer the sauce for 12–15 minutes to thicken it slightly. Pour over the plums and leave to cool a little before serving.

COCONUT MACAROONS

These sweet little cakes bring back memories of childhood – the little mountains of white desiccated coconut would be topped with a bright red cherry (although not on this diet!). These are less sweet but just as tasty.

MAKES 10–12

Prep time: 15 minutes
Cooking time: 15–18 minutes

1 tablespoon honey
20 g (¾ oz) coconut oil
275 g (9 oz) desiccated coconut
1 egg white

• Preheat the oven to 160°C (325°F), Gas Mark 3. Line a baking sheet with baking paper.

• Gently heat together the honey and coconut oil in a pan, then take the pan off the heat and allow the mixture to cool slightly before stirring in the desiccated coconut.

• Whisk the egg white until it forms soft peaks and fold in the coconut mixture.

• Fill an egg cup with the coconut mixture, pressing it down into the cup. Turn the egg cup over, and bang it into your hand to remove a perfectly formed dome-shape macaroon. Place the macaroon on to the prepared baking sheet and repeat with the remaining mixture.

• Bake for 15–16 minutes, until the macaroons are golden. Leave to cool on a wire rack before eating.

SWEET POTATO PUDDING

The original traditional sweet potato pudding recipe is made in Jamaica and includes brown sugar and rum. This recipe uses coconut flour, coconut milk and coconut oil, but remarkably is not overpowered by the coconut flavour because of the lovely spices and the hint of orange.

SERVES 6–8

Prep time: 12 minutes
Cooking time: 48–50 minutes

475 g (15 oz) sweet potato, chopped
2 oranges
3 eggs, whisked
200 ml (7 fl oz) coconut milk
50 g (2 oz) coconut oil, melted
2 tablespoons honey
½ teaspoons mixed spice
65 g (2½ oz) coconut flour
large pinch of grated nutmeg

• Preheat the oven to 180°C (350°F), Gas Mark 4.

• Cook the sweet potato in a pan of boiling water for 8–10 minutes, until tender. Drain and mash the potato and place it in a bowl to cool slightly.

• Grate the rind of both oranges. Whisk in the eggs, coconut milk, coconut oil, honey and mixed spice into the sweet potato mixture, along with the coconut flour and the grated orange rind.

• Pour the mixture into a 23 cm (9 inch) fluted flan tin, sprinkle with the grated nutmeg and bake for 40 minutes.

• Meanwhile, peel and segment the oranges.

• Serve the pudding, warm or cold, cut into wedges, with a few orange segments.

BAKED ALMOND AND GINGER PEACHES

Choose soft, ripe peaches for this sweet treat. You can also cook apricots or plums in the same way.

Serves 4

Prep time: 10 minutes
Cooking time: 20–22 minutes

2 knobs of stem ginger, diced
100 g (3½ oz) ground almonds
20 g (¾ oz) coconut oil
1 tablespoon clear honey
4 ripe peaches, halved and stoned

• Preheat the oven to 200°C (400°F), Gas Mark 6.

• Mix together the ginger, ground almonds, oil and honey in a bowl.

• Place the peaches, cut side up, in a roasting tin. Bake in the preheated oven for 10 minutes, then remove from the oven and spoon in the almond filling. Return to the oven and bake for a further 10–12 minutes until golden and soft.

• Serve the peaches drizzled with the pan juices.

PEAR AND ORANGE CRUMBLE WITH ALMOND CREAM

Just because you can't have dairy, doesn't mean you can't have cream. Here, nuts and non-dairy milk make an excellent cream equivalent.

SERVES 4

Prep time: 15 minutes
Cooking time: 20 minutes

4 pears, cored and sliced
1 orange
75 g (3 oz) ground almonds
25 g (1 oz) coconut oil
pinch of ground nutmeg
2 teaspoons clear honey
125 g (4 oz) blanched almonds
150 ml (¼ pint) non-dairy milk

- Preheated oven, 200°C (400°F) Gas Mark 6.

- Place the pears in a shallow ovenproof dish. Grate the rind of the orange into a separate bowl.

- Using a sharp knife, remove the peel and pith from the orange. Holding the orange over the pears to catch the juice, cut out the segments and add to the pears.

- Stir the ground almonds into the orange rind, then rub in the coconut oil, using the back of a spoon, until it resembles coarse breadcrumbs. Stir in the nutmeg.

- Sprinkle the crumble over the pears and drizzle with the honey. Bake in the preheated oven for 20 minutes.

- Meanwhile, place the blanched almonds in a food processor and blitz until finely ground. With the motor still running, gradually add the milk through the feeder tube until it forms a creamy consistency.

- Serve the crumble warm, with the almond cream.

INDEX